From **Evening** *to* **Morning**

Rediscovering ***GOD's Sacred Hours***

Gerard Assey

From Evening to Morning:
Rediscovering GOD's Sacred Hours

By

Gerard Assey

Published by:
Gerard Assey
19/18, Palli Arasan Street
Anna Nagar East
Chennai - 600 102

ISBN: 978-81-986974-3-1

Table of Contents

Preface

Time. We measure it by clocks, count it in hours, and chase it in our hurried lives. But somewhere along the way, we've forgotten that time is not just a commodity—it's a sacred gift. In the Scriptures, time pulses with divine rhythm. God doesn't move according to our busy schedules or digital calendars—He moves according to heaven's clock.

This book was born out of a yearning to rediscover what it means to live in sync with God's sacred hours. As I studied the Word, I noticed something curious: many of the most powerful moments in Scripture were not random. They happened at specific hours—12, 3, 6, 9—both day and night. These hours marked the movements of Jesus, the prayers of the apostles, the miracles of prophets, and the turning points of biblical history.

Then I looked at the clock faces in our homes and churches. Most of them emphasize these same four numbers—12, 3, 6, and 9. Was it just a design choice? Or could it be a divine reminder pointing us back to something we've forgotten?

The Jewish understanding of time, which begins at evening and flows into morning (Genesis 1), holds profound meaning. It teaches us that rest comes before work, and surrender comes before strength. It's a pattern that heaven still honors.

In a world that glorifies hustle and celebrates productivity, God is inviting us to live differently—to return to the ancient paths, the sacred rhythms, the stillness of the watches, and the power of appointed hours. This is not a call to superstition or ritualism, but to intentional relationship with the One who governs time.

This book is a journey through those hours. Each chapter is an open door into a moment where God meets us—when we pause, when we pray, when we align.

Whether you are a seasoned intercessor or just beginning to explore the idea of praying by divine rhythms, I pray that this book becomes a lamp to your path, a clock for your spirit, and a call back to the heartbeat of God.

Let us walk not by seconds and schedules alone, but by seasons and sacred moments.

Let us return—from evening to morning—to the God who calls us by the hour.

Chapter 1:
Time through GOD's Eyes

God's View of Time vs. Man's Time

We live in a world dominated by ticking clocks, digital calendars, deadlines, and scheduled meetings. Time, for us, is often mechanical—measured in hours, minutes, and seconds. From the moment we wake up to the moment we sleep, we're ruled by a system that starts the day at midnight and ends it just before the next one begins. But what if this isn't how God designed us to live? What if we've been following a rhythm that contradicts the very order God set in motion from the beginning?

To truly walk in alignment with Heaven, we must begin by seeing time through God's eyes.

Evening and Morning – The Divine Blueprint

The Bible opens not with chaos, but with divine order. In the creation account of Genesis 1, there's a repeated phrase that shapes God's view of time:

"And there was evening, and there was morning—the first day." (Genesis 1:5)

It's a phrase that appears six times, marking the completion of each creation day. Notice what it doesn't say—it doesn't say "morning and evening," but "evening and morning."

This is not a poetic accident. God, in His perfection, starts the day with evening, not morning. In the Hebrew mindset, which reflects God's original design, the day begins at sunset—a rhythm observed faithfully by the Jewish people even to this day.

This means that when God begins a new day, He starts it not with work, but with rest.

God's Day Begins with Rest

What a radical concept! Our world tells us to start with hustle—check emails, plan the day, rush out the door. But God says, "Start by resting in Me."

This idea isn't just symbolic—it reflects a deep spiritual truth: that life flows best when it begins from a place of surrender and trust. Just as Adam's first full day on earth was the Sabbath (Genesis 2:2-3)—a day of rest—we too are invited to live from rest into work, not the other way around.

Jesus echoed this rhythm in His own life. He often withdrew in the evening or early morning to pray (Mark 1:35, Luke 6:12). He understood that spiritual preparation happens before public ministry, that rest precedes revelation, and that night is not wasted time—it is sacred space.

Jewish Timekeeping vs. Roman Timekeeping

To understand this difference in worldview, let's contrast the two systems.

Jewish (Biblical) Timekeeping:

- ✓ Day begins at sunset (around 6:00 PM)
- ✓ Based on God's creation rhythm
- ✓ The day is divided into watches of the night and hours of the day
- ✓ Prioritizes rest, rhythm, and sacred time
- ✓ Sabbath is from Friday sunset to Saturday sunset

Roman (Modern) Timekeeping:

- ✓ Day begins at midnight (12:00 AM)
- ✓ Based on man-made systems and civil calendars
- ✓ Time is linear, secular, and detached from sacred meaning

- ✓ Work dominates the structure of the day
- ✓ Sabbath/Sunday becomes more symbolic than observed

Examples from the Bible
Old Testament

- ✓ **Genesis 1** sets the evening-first pattern.
- ✓ Exodus 12:6 – The Passover lamb was slain "at twilight," marking the start of a new sacred day.
- ✓ Leviticus 23:32 – The Day of Atonement is to be observed "from evening to evening."
- ✓ Nehemiah 13:19 – The gates of Jerusalem were shut as it grew dark before the Sabbath, showing the sacred time began at sunset.

New Testament

- ✓ Mark 15:42 – After Jesus' death, His body was taken down "because it was the preparation day, that is, the day before the Sabbath" (which began at sunset).
- ✓ Luke 24:29 – The disciples walking to Emmaus said, "Stay with us, for it is nearly evening; the day is almost over," acknowledging that the day ended at sunset.
- ✓ Acts 3:1 – Peter and John went to the temple "at the hour of prayer—the ninth hour (3 PM)," reflecting a sacred rhythm of prayer hours.

Real-Life Reflection: Living from Rest

I once spoke to a friend—a deeply spiritual woman—who shared how her breakthrough came not when she prayed more but when she began resting better. She said, "I realized I was trying to prove myself with my prayers instead of entering God's rest and trusting Him to work through me."

That struck me. How often do we think more activity equals more spirituality? But in God's economy, rest is not a pause from productivity—it's the starting point of purpose.

When we embrace God's view of time, we begin to see that rest is not laziness—it is trust. And we stop measuring our day by what we *did*, and instead by how much we *dwelt* in Him.

Why This Matters Today

In a culture obsessed with speed, performance, and noise, rediscovering God's sacred rhythm is not just refreshing—it's revolutionary.

When we align with God's timing, we:

- ✓ Prioritize presence over pressure
- ✓ Value quietness over busyness
- ✓ Learn to hear God better because we're not running ahead of Him
- ✓ Realize that life is not measured in hours, but in holy moments

Key Takeaway

- ✓ God sees time through the lens of purpose, not pressure.
- ✓ His day begins with rest, not rush.
- ✓ His time is sacred, not secular.
- ✓ And if we are to walk in sync with Him, we must relearn how to see time His way.

Prayer

Father, teach me to number my days according to Your heart. Help me to slow down and embrace Your rhythm of rest and purpose. May I no longer chase time, but walk in step with You—from evening to morning. Amen.

Chapter 2:
The 4 Corner Hours – 12, 3, 6, 9

Unlocking Heaven's Rhythm on Earth

Time has a face. And if you've ever stared at a classic clock, you know which numbers stand out the most. They're the four markers that divide the circle of time into quarters: 12, 3, 6, and 9. These aren't just design decisions made by clockmakers. In a way, they reveal a deeper rhythm—one that resonates not only in how we measure time but also in how God interacts with His people across time.

It is in these pivotal hours—noon, three, six, and nine—that we find not just historical markers, but spiritual invitations. Invitations to pause, reflect, connect, and realign with the One who holds time in His hands.

The Geometry of Time: Why These Hours Matter

Why are these four numbers emphasized on so many clocks? Why do they often stand alone while the others remain unnumbered or subtly marked? From a design perspective, they split the day into four quarters, helping us tell time at a glance. But from a spiritual perspective, they do something far more profound: they frame the gates of time.

Each quarter of the day carries with it a distinct spiritual tone, a history in Scripture, and even a psychological effect on our minds and bodies. The 12, 3, 6, and 9 positions are like hinges on a door—times when the heavens opened, prayers were answered, sacrifices were made, and divine power was revealed.

In Acts 3:1, we're told, *"Now Peter and John were going up to the temple at the hour of prayer—the ninth hour."* That's 3 PM. It wasn't just a convenient time. It was a sacred appointment—a rhythm the early Church continued from their Jewish heritage. And they knew, without a doubt, that heaven moves on rhythm, not just request.

Twelve O'Clock: The Midday Encounter

In the heat of the day, when most people would seek shelter or shade, Jesus met a woman at a well. *"It was about the sixth hour,"* John writes, referencing 12 noon by Jewish time (John 4:6). This moment, though ordinary by time's reckoning, was extraordinary in purpose. A Samaritan woman, bound by shame and secrecy, found herself face-to-face with the Messiah. In that blazing sun, truth was revealed, sin was uncovered, and destiny was rewritten.

Noon is not a quiet hour. It's when the day is loudest, brightest, and often most distracted. Yet, right in that noise, Jesus made room for encounter. This teaches us something powerful: God doesn't always wait for silence. Sometimes, He shows up in the middle of your messiest moment to speak truth.

Twelve also represents government and authority in Scripture—there were twelve tribes of Israel, twelve apostles, twelve gates in the New Jerusalem. It stands at the top of the clock for a reason. It marks divine rule **and** a call to alignment.

For us, midday is a chance to stop, recalibrate, and ask: *Am I still walking in step with God today? Or have I strayed under the heat of pressure and distraction?*

Three O'Clock: The Hour of Sacrifice and Power

There is no hour more significant than 3 PM in the narrative of our redemption. It was at this hour—the ninth hour in Jewish time—that Jesus gave up His spirit on the Cross (Matthew 27:46-50). His final cry, *"It is finished,"* wasn't just the end of a life—it was the breaking open of eternity for all humanity.

Darkness had covered the land since noon, but at three o'clock, light broke through the veil. Literally. The curtain in the temple was torn from top to bottom (Matthew 27:51), symbolizing that access to the Father was no longer reserved for priests behind a veil. Now, all who believed could come boldly to the throne of grace.

And this wasn't the only time 3 PM was sacred.

In Acts 3:1, as mentioned earlier, Peter and John were going up for prayer at the ninth hour. It was then they encountered the lame man at the temple gate—who was healed instantly in Jesus' name. This tells us something crucial: 3 PM is not only the hour of sacrifice—it is also the hour of supernatural power. For modern believers, this is a time to stop, remember, and reconnect with the finished work of the Cross. It's an hour to lay our burdens down and access the power of the risen Christ. Perhaps this is why intercessors often report breakthroughs in prayer during this sacred hour. Something in heaven shifts at 3 PM. Because something in history did.

Six O'Clock: The Divine Reset

According to Genesis 1, God counts a day from evening to evening. So when the sun begins to set, around 6 PM, a new day is beginning in heaven's calendar—even though it's the end of our workday here on earth.

This makes 6 PM the pivot of divine rhythm. It is not the end—it is the beginning of a fresh cycle. In Jewish tradition, this is when the Sabbath begins, ushered in with lighting of candles and blessings over the home. It's a time of peace, family, and presence.

Most people use 6 PM to wrap up work or turn to entertainment, but God invites us into something higher: rest and remembrance. Psalm 55:17 says, *"Evening and morning and at noon I will pray and cry aloud, and He shall hear my voice."* Evening comes first—because God starts the day with surrender, not striving.

Imagine how different our lives would be if we treated 6 PM not as the collapse of a long day, but the opening of a sacred one. What if, instead of zoning out, we zoned in—lighting a candle, pausing to pray, or eating with intentional gratitude? This hour resets our posture from self-reliance to rest in the Father's care.

Nine O'Clock: The Hour of Infilling and Purpose

When the Holy Spirit descended on the believers in the Upper Room, it was 9 AM, the third hour of the day (Acts 2:15). Peter stood and declared that what the crowd was witnessing wasn't drunkenness—it was fulfillment of prophecy.

This was the birthing hour of the Church.

This reminds us that God doesn't wait until the day has settled—He moves when the day is just beginning. At 9 AM, most people are busy launching into their routines, answering emails, sitting in meetings, or commuting to work. But in heaven's agenda, it's often a time of release and outpouring.

That moment in Acts wasn't random. The third hour was traditionally a time of prayer. The believers weren't just gathered—they were aligned. And when God found alignment, He poured Himself out.

This hour, for us, is a time to surrender our agenda and welcome His. It is the hour to say, *"Fill me today, Lord. Not with anxiety or ambition, but with Your Spirit and power."* Imagine starting each morning with a conscious request for the Holy Spirit to lead your day, just as He led the apostles.

The Clock Face: More Than Just Numbers

Now, look again at a simple wall clock. Those four numbers—12, 3, 6, 9—split time into sacred gates. They invite us to pause not just for practical reasons, but for spiritual purpose.

Each one offers a doorway:

- ✓ **12** calls you to **encounter**
- ✓ **3** calls you to **sacrifice and power**
- ✓ **6** calls you to **rest and renewal**
- ✓ **9** calls you to **infilling and alignment**

In a full day, you pass each of these gates twice—once in daylight, once in darkness. There's something beautiful about that. It means whether you're in the bright noon of success or the deep midnight of trial, God is present in all corners of time.

Scientific and Psychological Wisdom in Rhythms

Even science has begun to catch up with what Scripture has always known. Human beings function better in rhythmic patterns. Fixed points in a day give the brain a sense of security, focus, and emotional regulation. That's why prayer rhythms—like the ones followed by Daniel (Daniel 6:10), David (Psalm

55:17), or Jesus—are not just spiritual disciplines, but life-giving patterns.

Psychologists call it habit stacking—linking spiritual habits to specific times of day increases follow-through and joy. When you associate prayer with certain times, those hours become sacred appointments with God, not just items on a calendar.

Final Reflection

You don't need to overhaul your life to step into this rhythm. You just need to start by noticing time differently. Let 12, 3, 6, and 9 become more than digits. Let them become daily doors to divine encounters.

Heaven is not in a hurry, but it is incredibly timely. God doesn't rush, but He always moves at the right moment. And when we meet Him at those moments—when we pause, breathe, pray, and remember—we live not just in time, but in sync with eternity.

Lord, teach me to pause at the sacred gates of time. Help me to meet You at noon, at three, at six, and at nine—not out of ritual, but out of desire. May my life beat with the rhythm of heaven, and may I find You waiting at every quarter of my day. Amen.

Chapter 3:
6 PM – The Divine Reset

Why God Begins the Day at Evening

The world counts the day from midnight. But God, in His perfect wisdom, begins His day at sunset.

This singular truth, repeated like a refrain in the opening chapter of Genesis, has the power to change how we live, pray, and rest—if only we pay attention.

"And there was evening, and there was morning—the first day." —Genesis 1:5

Evening. Then morning. That is how God defines a day.

It's not a casual detail. It's a divine pattern—a declaration that before the work, before the tasks, before the pressures of performance, there is rest. A reset. A letting go.

And the hour that signals this divine reset, more often than not, is 6 PM.

A New Day Begins in the Dark

In our modern mindset, darkness is usually associated with endings. We say goodbye, close our laptops, pull down the blinds. But in the Hebrew worldview, darkness is not the end of the day—it is the beginning.

This can feel backwards to us, even uncomfortable. But that's because we've been conditioned by a system that measures time mechanically, not spiritually. The biblical view sees darkness not as the death of the day but as the womb of creation—the place where new things are formed, birthed, and spoken into existence.

Before light ever entered the scene, there was evening. And out of that evening, God spoke.

"The earth was without form, and void; and darkness was on the face of the deep... Then God said, 'Let there be light.'" —Genesis 1:2–3

Even in the beginning, God worked from darkness into light. So when the sun begins to set around 6 PM, we're not winding down—we're entering into a holy transition. The clock may say "the day is over," but heaven is saying, *"Welcome to the new day."*

Rest Is Not Lazy—It's Holy

There's a quiet holiness that settles in at dusk. It's the moment when the noise of the day starts to quiet down and the pace begins to slow. God didn't just ordain this as practical—He ordained it as sacred.

In Genesis 2:2-3, we are told that God rested on the seventh day, and then blessed the day and made it holy. The very first thing ever declared holy in Scripture was not a place or a person—it was a period of time, a space carved out specifically for rest.

"By the seventh day God had finished the work he had been doing; so on the seventh day he rested from all his work. Then God blessed the seventh day and made it holy..." —Genesis 2:2–3

In Hebrew culture, this holy day—Shabbat—begins on Friday evening at sunset, usually around 6 PM. The family gathers. Candles are lit. Blessings are spoken. Work ceases. And in that sacred pause, the presence of God is welcomed into the home.

It's not a burden; it's a gift.

Evening: The Time to Let Go

There's something spiritual about the evening hour. It's when we stand between what was and what's coming. Between the fatigue of the day and the unknown of tomorrow. If we're not careful, we'll carry today's burdens right into the next day's beginning.

That's why 6 PM is so significant. It's God's way of saying: *"You don't need to carry this into the next chapter. Let it go."*

The psalmist captured this rhythm beautifully:

"In peace I will lie down and sleep, for you alone, O Lord, make me dwell in safety." —Psalm 4:8

This is not just about physical sleep. It's about spiritual release—a letting go of anxiety, offense, pressure, and even success. At 6 PM, we begin again. But we don't start with doing. We start with trust.

Jesus and the Evening Rhythm

Jesus honored the evening hour. In fact, some of His most significant moments unfolded as the day closed.

In Luke 24:29, after the resurrection, the disciples on the road to Emmaus urged Jesus to stay with them, saying: *"Stay with us, for it is nearly evening; the day is almost over."* It was at that table, in the quiet of the evening, that Jesus broke the bread and revealed Himself to them.

Even His final meal—the Last Supper—took place in the evening (Matthew 26:20). And after it, He withdrew to the garden to pray.

There's something in the stillness of evening that makes room for deeper communion. When the noise of the world fades, our ears become more tuned to the whispers of heaven.

Real Life: From Burnout to Breath

I remember speaking with a friend who used to wear his productivity like a badge of honor. Every evening, he'd work late into the night—emails, calls, reports—until he collapsed into bed exhausted, only to wake up dreading the next day.

One evening, after a near breakdown, he sensed the Lord speak softly to him: *"You've been living outside My rhythm."*

He began doing something simple. At 6 PM each evening, he'd shut off work, light a candle, and spend just ten minutes in silence before God. Sometimes he'd pray. Sometimes he'd just breathe. But every night, it became his divine reset. Over time, he noticed his sleep improved, his anxiety decreased, and his sense of connection to God deepened.

It wasn't the silence itself that changed him. It was the surrender.

Sacred Practices at 6 PM

So how do we reclaim 6 PM as sacred?

It starts with intentionality. You don't need incense or rituals. Just a heart that's willing to stop and say, *"Lord, I trust You with what's behind me and what's ahead."*

This could look like:

- ✓ Turning off your phone for a while.
- ✓ Lighting a candle as a symbol of divine presence.
- ✓ Praying over your family or meal.
- ✓ Reading a psalm aloud.
- ✓ Simply sitting in silence and whispering, *"Thank You, Lord. I give You this day."*

In doing so, you align with the rhythm of creation. You step out of culture's pressure and into the cadence of the Creator.

A Holy Invitation

Each day, God extends an invitation at sunset. It's not an invitation to do more, but to do less. To cease striving. To breathe. To trust. To hand the day back to the One who wrote it.

The world tells you that the day is almost done at 6 PM. But heaven tells you, *it's just beginning.*

When we begin the day with rest, we declare to the world—and to ourselves—that God is in control, not us. That His grace is sufficient. That His power is made perfect in our surrender.

That's the beauty of 6 PM.

Closing Prayer

Lord, as the sun sets and the day begins in Your eyes, help me to enter Your rest. I surrender the outcomes, the anxieties, the mistakes, and the victories of this day. Teach me to begin from stillness, not from striving. Let my evenings become sacred spaces where I meet with You, where peace returns, and where trust is renewed. In Jesus' name, Amen.

Chapter 4:
9 PM – The Night Watch

When Heaven Keeps Vigil and Earth Must Respond

As the evening deepens and the world around us begins to retreat into quietness, we find ourselves approaching the 9 PM hour. For many, this is when lights are dimmed, screens are scrolled, minds are numbed, and bodies prepare for sleep. But in God's timekeeping, 9 PM marks the first night watch—a sacred hour when the soul is most open, heaven is alert, and the Spirit begins to whisper louder than the noise of the day.

The ancients didn't view night as a passive pause between two days. In Scripture, the night was alive with divine activity—a time of revelation, visitation, and warfare. And the 9 PM watch, beginning what the Hebrews referred to as the First Watch of the Night, was the gateway into that sacred space.

A Time Appointed for Watchers

In biblical times, the Jews divided the night into three watches: from 6–10 PM, 10 PM–2 AM, and 2–6 AM. The Romans later adjusted this into four watches of three hours each. The first Roman watch, then, began at 6 PM and ended at 9 PM; the second started at 9 PM and ran to midnight.

By 9 PM, the busyness of the day had faded. Dinner was done. The household quieted. It was a time when shepherds would keep watch, when soldiers would be stationed, and when prophets would begin to receive visions.

This was not an idle hour—it was an hour of keeping vigil. A moment where the faithful watched with expectation, listened with discernment, and prayed with persistence.

"I rise before dawn and cry for help; I have put my hope in Your word. My eyes stay open through the watches of the night, that I may meditate on Your promises."

—Psalm 119:147–148

David didn't speak these words as a poetic exaggeration. He meant them. He literally stayed awake during the night watches, not because of anxiety, but because his soul was hungry—longing for the voice and presence of God. At 9 PM, his heart had already begun its vigil.

Jesus and the First Watch

Jesus Himself honored this pattern. One of the clearest examples comes in the Gethsemane account. After the Last Supper—held in the evening—He led His disciples to the garden. By the time He told them to "stay here and watch with Me," it was likely approaching 9 PM (Matthew 26:36–40).

What followed was a picture of what so often happens to us. While Jesus agonized in prayer, preparing to drink the bitter cup of suffering, His disciples did the very thing we are often tempted to do at night: they fell asleep.

"Could you not watch with Me for one hour?" Jesus asked Peter. —Matthew 26:40

It wasn't just a rebuke. It was an invitation.

9 PM is not just for rest—it is for watchfulness. In the silence of night, Jesus longed for companionship in prayer. The first watch is about attentiveness—not

just to what we need, but to what He desires to share with us.

The Spiritual Significance of 9 PM

In Scripture, darkness often symbolizes trial or temptation. But it also marks the place where God begins to move in unseen ways. Think of Ruth, who lay quietly at the feet of Boaz during the night (Ruth 3). Think of Samuel, who heard the voice of the Lord calling him while lying in the temple during the watches (1 Samuel 3:3–10). Think of Paul and Silas, who were praying and singing hymns at midnight in prison—likely beginning their songs around this very hour (Acts 16:25).

At 9 PM, the distractions of the world are finally low enough for divine whispers to be heard. It's when the body may be winding down, but the spirit is waking up.

This is also a time of spiritual warfare. The enemy loves darkness—he thrives in it. But Scripture teaches us to watch and pray so that we do not fall into temptation (Mark 14:38). The night watch is about being alert—not fearful, but faithful.

Psalm 91 speaks of those who dwell in the secret place of the Most High. It promises that we will not fear "the terror by night" (Psalm 91:5). But that fearlessness is only possible when we abide, when we dwell in that secret place—and the night is often where that dwelling is tested.

Prayer and Meditation Before Bed

It's far too easy to let Netflix or scrolling through a phone be the last thing that touches our mind before sleep. But what we engage with in this hour seeps into our subconscious. The soul is impressionable just before sleep—what we meditate on in this hour often determines the tone of our rest and the clarity of our dreams.

The psalmist knew this well:

"On my bed I remember You; I think of You through the watches of the night. Because You are my help, I sing in the shadow of Your wings." —Psalm 63:6–7

There is something holy about ending your day in the arms of God's presence. Whether through whispered prayers, the reading of a psalm, or simply being still before Him, 9 PM becomes a threshold between the conscious and the unconscious. A gate into which we can invite God's peace to guard our hearts and minds.

Real-Life Reflection: Night as Sanctuary

A young woman once shared with me how she struggled with insomnia, anxiety, and intrusive thoughts. She tried all the practical remedies—diet, supplements, even white noise—but nothing helped. Then one night, she began a simple practice. At 9 PM, she turned off her lights, lit a single candle, and read a portion of Scripture aloud. She would then kneel beside her bed and pray—sometimes just for five minutes.

What began as a discipline soon became her lifeline. Her sleep deepened. Her dreams became clearer. And more importantly, her heart became settled.

She said, *"The night stopped feeling like a threat and started feeling like a sanctuary."*

This is what 9 PM is meant to be—a spiritual reset, not just a physical routine. A time to let go of control, offer your soul to God, and prepare to receive divine rest.

Protection in the Night Watch

The 9 PM hour is not only for intimacy—it is also for intercession and protection.

When the Israelites prepared to leave Egypt, God gave specific instructions for the night of Passover. At evening, they were to slaughter the lamb, mark their doorposts with its blood, and eat in haste (Exodus 12:6–11). That night, as darkness fell, the angel of death passed over the houses covered by the blood.

It was during the night watch that deliverance came—and also judgment.

There's a reason why many intercessors and prayer warriors feel compelled to pray during the night. Because much spiritual battle takes place when the world sleeps. But those who are awake in the Spirit, who pray and declare the Word of God over their homes, families, and nations, are participating in heaven's defense strategy.

"Unless the Lord watches over the city, the watchman stays awake in vain." —Psalm 127:1

At 9 PM, we step into that role—not as anxious people hoping to fend off darkness, but as priests standing guard over the territory God has entrusted to us.

A Sacred Closing to the Day

If 6 PM is the divine reset, then 9 PM is the holy seal—the prayerful placing of your day in God's hands.

You can pray:

"Lord, thank You for this day. Thank You for what I saw, and what You protected me from. I release every care to You now."

"Guard my mind and my dreams. Speak to me as I sleep."
"Protect this house, my family, and my heart from any assignment of the enemy."
"Let Your presence dwell here, even in the dark."
What happens at 9 PM sets the tone for the rest of the night. Will your sleep be filled with stress or peace? Will your dreams be chaotic or prophetic? Will you lay down in fear or faith?

Closing Reflection

At 9 PM, the world may think the day is over. But for those who walk in God's rhythm, it's just the beginning of a sacred watch. It's the hour when lovers of God stay awake a little longer—not just physically, but spiritually. It's when hearts are still enough to hear His voice, and strong enough to contend for what matters most.
So tonight, when the clock strikes nine, don't just scroll. Don't just collapse. **Watch. Wait. Listen. Pray.**
Because Heaven is awake.
And God is watching with you.

Lord, as the night stretches before me, help me to stay awake in my spirit. Let the 9 PM hour be my watchtower, my place of peace, and my point of connection with You. Cover me with Your feathers. Guard my thoughts. Set angels at the gates. And let my night be filled with Your presence. In Jesus' name, Amen.

Chapter 5:
12 AM – The Midnight Cry

When Darkness Meets Divine Intervention

Midnight is a strange hour. It's the deep middle of the night when most of the world is asleep, unaware, and unguarded. The streets fall silent. The lights dim. Even the air feels different—still, eerie, charged. In our modern, mechanical reckoning of time, 12 AM marks the start of a new day. But in God's economy, it is more than the flipping of a calendar—it is an hour of divine intervention, disruption, and often, deliverance.

For some, midnight is merely a number on the clock. But for those attuned to the Spirit, it has long been known as the hour when heaven responds to earth's desperate cry.

The Mystery of Midnight in Scripture

All throughout the Bible, midnight is a spiritual intersection—a time when God chooses to move with force, clarity, and often, surprise. It is when the unseen realm becomes active, when chains are broken, and when God answers cries that have been simmering in prayer and perseverance.

The first major example comes straight out of the Exodus:

"And it came to pass at midnight that the Lord struck all the firstborn in the land of Egypt…" —Exodus 12:29

This was not just a historical moment—it was a divine turning point. For over four hundred years, Israel had been enslaved. They had cried, groaned, and suffered under Pharaoh's oppression. But at midnight, God moved decisively. That very night, Pharaoh called Moses and Aaron and said, *"Go, serve the Lord!"* (Exodus 12:31). Their deliverance came suddenly, but not randomly—it came strategically, at midnight.

Why midnight? Perhaps because midnight is the breaking point—that final moment before the darkest hour surrenders to dawn. It's when human strength ends, and only divine power can do what needs to be done.

Paul and Silas: Praise at Midnight

One of the most dramatic New Testament examples of the midnight hour is found in Acts 16.

Paul and Silas had been beaten, chained, and thrown into the innermost prison. Every natural reason to despair surrounded them. But what did they do?

"But at midnight Paul and Silas were praying and singing hymns to God, and the prisoners were listening to them." —Acts 16:25

Midnight became their altar of praise. They weren't waiting for a breakthrough to worship—they worshipped into their breakthrough. And suddenly—midnight again—a violent earthquake shook the prison, the doors flew open, and every chain was loosed.

At midnight, their worship became a weapon. Their prison became a platform for the gospel. And their endurance became a testimony that still speaks centuries later.

The Midnight Cry of the Bridegroom

In Matthew 25, Jesus shares a parable that begins with a waiting community—a group of virgins waiting for the Bridegroom. All of them had lamps. But not all had oil.

And when did the Bridegroom come?

"At midnight a cry was heard: 'Behold, the bridegroom is coming; go out to meet him!'" —Matthew 25:6

The midnight cry wasn't just a sound in the dark—it was a call to readiness. And only those who were prepared responded well.

This story isn't about oil and lamps alone. It's about how we live when we think no one is watching. Midnight is the time when true character is revealed. It's when the slumbering world is caught unaware, and only those who have cultivated a life of spiritual alertness will rise to meet the moment.

In many ways, midnight is not just a moment on the clock—it is a spiritual metaphor. It reminds us that Jesus could come at a time we least expect. And that, in the deepest darkness, the greatest glory may suddenly appear.

Midnight Intercession: When Heaven Hears the Hidden Cry

There's something raw and desperate about praying at midnight. It's not the time for polished words or rehearsed phrases. It's the hour when your soul groans, when you whisper things you wouldn't say in daylight, when your heart is laid bare before God.

In Lamentations 2:19, Jeremiah gives this urgent instruction:

"Arise, cry out in the night, at the beginning of the watches; pour out your heart like water before the face of the Lord."

There's something powerful about that phrase: *pour out your heart like water*. Not trickle. Not measure. But pour.

Midnight prayer is not about elegance—it is about desperation. And desperation has always moved the heart of God.

Many revivals in history began when just a few people gathered in secret, at night, crying out for God to move. Midnight intercessors may never preach on stages, but they shift things in the heavens.

Testimonies of the Midnight Watch

A man once shared with me how his life changed because of midnight prayer. He had been battling years of addiction—hidden, silent, tormenting. He had tried therapy, support groups, even self-help routines. But one night, after everyone was asleep, he fell to his knees at 12 AM and cried out to God—not with structured words, but with brokenness.

He did it again the next night. And the next. He began keeping a journal of his midnight cries. They were sometimes wordless. Sometimes filled with anger. Sometimes tears. But night after night, something began to shift. One day, without realizing it, he had gone three weeks without falling back into the old pattern.

When I asked him what changed, he said, *"The chains didn't fall off at once. But every midnight, I left another one at His feet."*

That is the power of the midnight cry. It is not always a moment—it is often a process of surrender that culminates in breakthrough.

From Crisis to Cry to Calm

Sometimes, midnight comes not because we're praying, but because we're in crisis. The diagnosis arrives late. The betrayal unfolds when the world is sleeping. The worst phone calls come when your heart is unguarded and your soul is fragile.

And in those moments, when the world cannot help, God invites us to cry to Him.

Psalm 119:62 declares:

"At midnight I rise to give You thanks for Your righteous laws."

Not to complain. Not to beg. To give thanks. Because even at midnight, He is righteous. Even in the deepest darkness, His Word is true.

What Midnight Teaches Us

Midnight teaches us that God is not restricted by human logic or daylight. He doesn't wait for perfect conditions. He moves in the dark. He speaks in the stillness. He delivers in the depth of night.

Midnight teaches us to:

- ✓ Stay ready, *like the wise virgins with oil.*
- ✓ Keep praising, *like Paul and Silas, even when shackled.*
- ✓ Cry out, *like the Israelites in bondage, knowing He hears.*
- ✓ Pour out, *like Jeremiah urged, when your heart has no words.*
- ✓ Expect suddenly, *because God often moves at the darkest point.*

Final Thoughts

12 AM is not just a transition point on the clock—it is a threshold. The veil between heaven and earth feels thinner. The room becomes a sanctuary. The silence

becomes sacred. And the cry of your heart becomes a catalyst for the supernatural.

Whether you whisper in prayer, sit in silence, sing through tears, or simply kneel in surrender—God is near at midnight.

He doesn't slumber. He doesn't sleep. And when His people cry out in the dark, He answers in power.

Prayer at the Midnight Hour

Lord, this midnight, I come not with polished words, but with a broken heart. I cry to You from the deep places. Let this hour be holy. Let chains break. Let doors open. Let peace descend. You are the God of midnight miracles. So I wait, I watch, and I worship. In Jesus' name, Amen.

Chapter 6:
3 AM – The Fourth Watch

When Heaven Walks into the Storm

There's something hauntingly sacred about 3 AM. It's that silent hour when the world is shrouded in sleep and the darkness feels thick and heavy. But for those who have been awakened in this hour—not by noise, but by Spirit—there's a knowing deep inside that this time is not ordinary. It's charged. Stirring. Holy.

The ancient world divided the night into four watches. The Fourth Watch, from 3 AM to 6 AM, was the final guard of the night—the threshold of dawn. Roman soldiers took shifts during these watches, but so did heaven. In fact, some of Scripture's most remarkable encounters, breakthroughs, and revelations took place precisely during this window.

It's as though the Lord saves His deepest movements for when the world is deepest in slumber.

Jesus Walking on the Water: A Fourth Watch Miracle

In one of the most breathtaking moments in the Gospels, we find Jesus defying natural law, walking toward His disciples on the water in the pitch of night.

"Now in the fourth watch of the night Jesus went to them, walking on the sea." —Matthew 14:25

They had been rowing against a fierce wind, battling the waves for hours. Exhausted. Frustrated. Alone. And just when the night was about to give way to morning, He came.

He didn't arrive when the storm began. He didn't come in the first watch when the fear set in, nor in the second or third when their arms were already sore and their hopes fading. He came in the fourth watch—at 3 AM, when they had nothing left but fatigue and confusion.

And how did He come? Walking calmly on the very thing that terrified them.

This is the heartbeat of the 3 AM hour. It is the time when Jesus walks into our storms, not with loud announcements or obvious answers, but in supernatural stillness. He moves toward us when we think He's forgotten, and sometimes, like the disciples, we don't even recognize Him at first.

"They cried out in fear, thinking it was a ghost." — Matthew 14:26

But Jesus immediately said to them, *"Take courage. It is I. Do not be afraid."*

The fourth watch is a place of revelation. It's where we discover who Jesus really is—not just a teacher or healer, but Lord of the storm, Master of wind and wave.

Heaven's Watchtower: The Most Spiritually Active Time

Many spiritual leaders, prophets, and intercessors through the ages have identified 3 AM as the most spiritually active hour of the day. Not because of superstition, but because of Scripture and experience.

Why? Because it is the hour where night begins to lose its grip. It's the turning of the tide. The hour where darkness is still thick—but losing. The hour where God often chooses to release angelic activity, prophetic dreams, divine instructions, and unseen breakthroughs.

It was during the early watches of the morning that Jacob wrestled with the angel (Genesis 32:24-30). The match continued through the night until the breaking of day—again, around this fourth watch. It wasn't just a fight; it was a spiritual transformation. Jacob came away limping—but he came away with a new name, a new identity, and a fresh anointing.

So many today are wrestling at 3 AM—with anxiety, with fear, with decisions, with pain. But they don't realize what Jacob learned: sometimes the wrestling is the doorway to the blessing.

Prophetic Dreams and Divine Downloads

God has always spoken through dreams. From Joseph in Egypt to Daniel in Babylon, to Joseph the earthly father of Jesus—the night hours were a canvas for heaven's communication.

"In the last days, God says, I will pour out my Spirit… your old men will dream dreams, your young men will see visions." —Joel 2:28

What's interesting is that many who walk closely with God often find their most profound dreams happening between 2 and 4 AM. They describe dreams that are vivid, clear, and loaded with symbolism. They wake up with insights, direction, and sometimes, deep conviction.

A friend of mine, a pastor and worship leader, once shared how she kept waking up at exactly 3:07 AM for several nights in a row. The third time it happened, she felt the Holy Spirit say, *"Get up. I'm speaking."* She opened her Bible to Jeremiah 3:7, not knowing what it said.

"I thought that after she had done all this she would return to Me. But she did not…"

It was a word for her church, which had been coasting in lukewarmness. That 3 AM encounter birthed a season of repentance, worship, and a renewed hunger in their congregation.

The 3 AM hour is not just mystical—it is missional. God uses it to call His people into alignment, repentance, or preparation. If you're being stirred awake during these hours, don't ignore it. He may be placing you on a heavenly assignment.

When Warfare Intensifies

There is no denying that spiritual warfare peaks at night, particularly around the fourth watch. It's when people often experience nightmares, oppression, or a sense of unseen battle.

The enemy loves the cover of darkness. But Scripture reminds us that the God who keeps Israel does not slumber nor sleep (Psalm 121:4). He is active. Watching. Protecting. And empowering His people to war in the Spirit.

The apostle Peter tells us:

"Be alert and of sober mind. Your enemy the devil prowls around like a roaring lion looking for someone to devour." —1 Peter 5:8

That's why prayer during the fourth watch is so critical. It isn't only intercession—it's intervention. It's asking God to rise up, to scatter darkness, to open the heavens over your home, family, church, and community.

Many deliverance ministers pray during the 3 AM hour for exactly this reason: to confront demonic activity, to release captives, and to stand guard as spiritual watchmen over the city.

You don't have to shout. You don't need a crowd. You just need to be awake and willing. Because when the church sleeps, the enemy creeps. But when the saints rise up in the night, hell trembles.

Real-Life Awakening: When God Calls by Name

I once met a young man who had left the faith, diving into destructive habits and intellectual rebellion. One night, around 3 AM, he suddenly awoke with a pounding heart and a sense that someone had spoken his name out loud.

He looked around. No one there. But the room felt charged with presence. And he began to weep uncontrollably. He said it was as though his soul remembered God, even though his mind had been running from Him.

That 3 AM awakening marked the beginning of his return to Christ. Not through a sermon or song—but through an unshakable encounter in the fourth watch.

This is what the fourth watch does. It interrupts. It awakens. It speaks. It saves.

The Dawn Is Near

Perhaps the most powerful truth of the 3 AM hour is this: it means the night is almost over. Dawn is close. So many times in our lives we feel like the darkness will last forever. The pain. The silence. The waiting. But if you're awake at 3 AM, you're standing in the most fragile, beautiful hour—the hour before breakthrough.

"Weeping may endure for a night, but joy comes in the morning." —Psalm 30:5

God doesn't waste night hours. And He certainly doesn't waste the fourth watch.

A Watchman's Prayer at 3 AM

Lord, this is the hour where I have no strength of my own. I come empty, but expectant. Speak to me in the silence. Walk toward me in the storm. Breathe on me as I wait. Let this watch be holy. Let this hour be filled with divine movement. I stand as a watchman. Let me hear what You are saying. Let me dream what You are revealing. And let Your presence fill the darkness. In Jesus' name, Amen.

Chapter 7:
6 AM – Morning with the Master

The Dawn of Divine Alignment

There is something sacred about the morning—when the sky slowly bleeds from black to blue, when dew settles quietly on the grass, and when the first light breaks through the silence of night. It is the hour where God's mercies are made new, where the soul exhales, and where the day stands before you like an unpainted canvas. And at the center of this stillness is an invitation from the Master: *"Come. Sit with Me. Begin with Me."*

For those who have learned to walk closely with the Lord, 6 AM is more than just another hour. It is the portal through which purpose enters. The hour that, if embraced with faith, has the power to reshape the entire day.

Morning Devotions and New Mercies

The Scriptures speak softly but powerfully about mornings. Not just as a time of day, but as a symbol of new beginnings, divine favor, and fresh alignment.

"Because of the Lord's great love we are not consumed, for His compassions never fail. They are new every morning; great is Your faithfulness." — Lamentations 3:22–23

Imagine that: *new mercies*—not recycled, not rationed, but new. At 6 AM, we don't just wake to another routine; we awaken to a God who renews His commitment to us, who offers forgiveness for yesterday's failures and grace for today's unknowns.

Many people live with a sense of dread about the day ahead. The emails. The deadlines. The demands of life. But morning with the Master reminds us that we don't enter the day alone. We rise in the presence of the One who already knows what's coming—and already has a plan for it.

The psalmist understood this when he declared:

"In the morning, Lord, You hear my voice; in the morning I lay my requests before You and wait expectantly." —Psalm 5:3

This is what morning devotion truly is—not an obligation, but an offering. A moment to lay everything—our hopes, fears, to-do lists, and questions—before God, and to wait not in anxiety, but in expectancy.

Jesus' Early Morning Rhythm

If there's anyone who didn't "need" prayer, it was Jesus. And yet, we see Him repeatedly slipping away at dawn to be with the Father.

"Very early in the morning, while it was still dark, Jesus got up, left the house and went off to a solitary place, where He prayed." —Mark 1:35

The context of this passage is powerful. The day before had been filled with miracles—healing the sick, casting out demons, teaching the multitudes. He could have used the morning to rest or recharge. Instead, He rose early to realign. Because even Jesus, in His humanity, knew the importance of staying in sync with the Father.

He didn't start with activity—He started with abiding.

This rhythm of rising early to pray wasn't a one-time act. Luke tells us that Jesus *"often withdrew to lonely places and prayed"* (Luke 5:16). It was His lifestyle. His rhythm. And perhaps His secret.

If Jesus, the Son of God, needed early-morning communion with the Father, how much more do we?

Aligning Your Workday with God's Will

Most of us start our mornings in a frenzy. Alarms. Showers. Children. Commutes. Coffee. We often step into the day like we're jumping onto a moving train—already late, already behind.

But when we meet God at 6 AM, something changes. The day no longer controls us—we partner with it. We don't react; we respond. We don't strive; we surrender.

Jesus taught His disciples to pray, *"Your kingdom come, Your will be done, on earth as it is in heaven"* (Matthew 6:10). When we pray this first thing in the morning, we are not only surrendering our own will; we are inviting heaven's order into our earthly responsibilities.

Think of the Israelites gathering manna in the wilderness. It came fresh every morning, but it had to be collected early—before the sun grew hot and it melted away (Exodus 16:21). Morning was their provision window. If they waited too long, they missed it.

Likewise, there is a window of divine wisdom and favor that often opens in the early hours—a download of clarity, strength, or strategy that helps us face the day with peace and purpose.

Real-Life Stories: Where the Morning Changed Everything

I once met a young executive who told me he used to start his mornings by scrolling through emails and news updates. "It was like I was feeding my soul poison before I even left the house," he confessed. Stress followed him into every meeting. Anger simmered under the surface.

Then one day, out of sheer desperation, he decided to wake up an hour earlier and begin with God. No phones. No news. Just his Bible, a journal, and a cup of coffee at 6 AM.

What happened wasn't instant, but it was undeniable. "Peace started to guard me," he said. "I stopped reacting. I started listening. My decisions got clearer. My staff noticed a difference before I even told them what had changed."

He didn't become perfect. But he became anchored. And that's what the morning watch does—it anchors your soul before the storm begins.

Sunrise Encounters in Scripture

Scripture is dotted with sacred morning moments—divine whispers carried on the breeze of dawn.

- ✓ Abraham rose early to obey God (Genesis 22:3).
- ✓ Jacob, after wrestling with the angel through the night, saw God face-to-face *"as the sun rose"* (Genesis 32:31).
- ✓ Moses rose early and ascended Sinai to meet with God (Exodus 34:4).
- ✓ Job offered sacrifices for his children *early in the morning* (Job 1:5), interceding for their hearts before they even woke up.

Morning wasn't just a time slot. It was a sacred meeting place. A pattern of prioritizing God above all else.

The Invitation of Dawn

Each morning is a grace-laced invitation. Not just to breathe, but to begin with the One who gave us breath.

The enemy would love for us to begin our day distracted, distressed, or indifferent. But when we begin with God—at 6 AM, in stillness, before the world pulls at us—we take authority over the atmosphere of the day. We declare, *"This day belongs to the Lord, and I will walk it with Him."*

You don't need to be eloquent. You don't need hours. Even fifteen intentional minutes of prayer, Scripture reading, and quiet listening can change the course of your day—and, over time, your life.

Closing Prayer: Morning with the Master

Lord, as the sun rises, so does my soul to meet You. Thank You for Your new mercies today. I offer You my thoughts, my steps, my desires. Align me with Your will. Fill me with Your Spirit. Let this morning be holy—not just in silence, but in surrender. As I go into the world, go before me. Walk beside me. Speak through me. And bring me back to You at day's end. In Jesus' name, Amen.

Chapter 8:
9 AM – The Spirit Hour

The Wind That Starts the Day

There are hours that pass quietly, unnoticed. And then there are hours where the world shifts—where heaven meets earth in a way that forever marks human history.

9 AM is one such hour.

For many of us, 9 AM marks the true start of the day. The rush to the office settles. Coffee is half-empty. The phone starts ringing. It's the hour when the world expects us to get to work. But in the Kingdom of God, this hour carries something far weightier than business meetings or inboxes. It is a sacred time—the hour of divine empowerment. The Spirit Hour.

It was at 9 AM that the world was introduced to a new era—not of religion, but of relationship. Not of mere belief, but of power. An hour where weak people became bold. Where ordinary men began speaking in heavenly tongues. Where the Church was born, not in a cathedral, but in an upper room filled with fire.

The Outpouring in Acts 2: A Morning That Changed the World

We can never understand the weight of 9 AM without revisiting that upper room in Jerusalem.

After Jesus ascended, He told His disciples to wait in the city until they received power from on high (Luke 24:49). They didn't know when or how it would come—they only knew *Who* was coming.

And then it happened.

"When the day of Pentecost came, they were all together in one place. Suddenly a sound like the blowing of a violent wind came from heaven…" — Acts 2:1–2

Tongues of fire. Mighty wind. Holy boldness. Languages they had never learned. Fear melted into confidence. Confusion turned into clarity. The Spirit had come—not just to visit—but to dwell within them.

And when the crowds gathered in amazement, questioning what was happening, Peter stood up and declared:

"These men are not drunk, as you suppose. It's only the third hour of the day!" —Acts 2:15

The third hour—by Jewish timekeeping—was 9 AM.

This was no coincidence. God chose 9 AM, the hour of the morning sacrifice in the Temple, to pour out His Spirit on living temples—His people. It was no longer about burnt offerings. The fire was now on their heads. The wind wasn't passing through a veil in the Holy of Holies—it was blowing through their hearts.

9 AM became the birthing hour of the Church—when ordinary people became empowered witnesses.

Empowerment for Your Mission

The beauty of Acts 2 isn't just that it happened. It's that it still happens.

The same Spirit that fell at 9 AM that morning now lives in you. And every morning, you and I have a choice: to enter the day in our own strength, or to yield and let Him lead.

The Spirit Hour is not about a ritual—it's about relationship, readiness, and release.

Think of Peter. Just days earlier, he had denied Jesus in fear. But at 9 AM on Pentecost, that same man stood in front of thousands and preached with fire. The only difference? The Spirit.

When you start your day in the Spirit, you're not just getting through life—you're stepping into mission. You're walking into meetings with discernment. You're talking to colleagues with compassion. You're facing challenges with wisdom beyond your education. Because the Holy Spirit isn't just your comforter—He's your power source.

Real-Life Reflection: The CEO and the Chair

A business leader once shared how he had completely restructured his mornings. Instead of diving straight into emails or news, he would begin his workday with ten minutes of sitting in silence before God, right in his office. No agenda. No requests. Just, *"Holy Spirit, lead this day."*

He placed an empty chair next to him as a visual reminder of the Spirit's presence.

Over time, he began to notice something unusual. Clarity came quicker. Difficult conversations became peaceful. Strategic decisions flowed with less strain. One day he said to me, *"I've learned more from ten quiet minutes with the Spirit than I have in a month of strategy meetings."*

He wasn't trying to be spiritual. He was just learning to live Spirit-led at 9 AM, where purpose begins.

The Hour of Direction and Divine Appointments

Scripture shows us that Spirit-led mornings often lead to divine encounters.

In Acts 3, Peter and John were on their way to the temple at the hour of prayer—again, 9 AM—when they encountered the man at the Beautiful Gate.

What began as a routine walk turned into a miracle moment.
"Silver and gold I do not have, but what I do have I give you…" (Acts 3:6)
That's the power of 9 AM when aligned with the Spirit—you're no longer reacting to life; you're releasing heaven into it.
And that's what the Spirit does best. He leads you into divine appointments—conversations you didn't plan, encounters that bear fruit, moments that change atmospheres. But you have to be tuned in.
That's why this hour matters. 9 AM is the point where the day truly takes off. And unless we begin anchored in the Spirit, we risk being swept into the rush of flesh-driven decisions.

What Would Happen If...
What would happen if believers across the world stopped every day at 9 AM—even for five minutes—to surrender to the Spirit?
Imagine if offices, schools, homes, construction sites—paused for just a moment to whisper: *"Holy Spirit, guide me now. Empower me. Use me."*
He would respond. He always does. Because He's not waiting for perfect conditions—He's just waiting for willing vessels.

The Spirit Is Willing—Are You?
The 9 AM hour confronts us with a question we cannot avoid: Will I lead my day, or will I let the Spirit lead me?
It's tempting to move fast. To get efficient. To rely on experience. But Acts 2 reminds us: even the best preparation falls short without the power of God.

You were never meant to do life in your own strength. You were made to be Spirit-filled, Spirit-empowered, and Spirit-led. And 9 AM is your chance to start again.

Whether you work in a boardroom or a kitchen, whether you teach, sell, write, lead, or build—you carry the same Spirit that raised Christ from the dead. And He is eager to anoint the work of your hands.

Closing Prayer: Breath of the Morning

Holy Spirit, I welcome You into this day. As the world begins to move, I choose to begin with You. Fall fresh on me. Guide my decisions. Empower my words. Use my hands. Let Your wind fill my lungs and Your fire ignite my heart. I don't want to walk ahead of You, nor behind You—I want to walk with You. This day belongs to You. Lead me. In Jesus' name, Amen.

Chapter 9:
12 PM – The Hour of Encounter

When Heaven Meets the Weary Soul

For many, 12 PM marks the middle of the day. The engine of life is in full motion—phones buzzing, meetings rolling, traffic increasing, to-do lists still half-complete. It's a moment that often rushes past unnoticed, devoured by deadlines and noise.

And yet, midday carries a rhythm of divine interruption.

When the clock strikes twelve, something subtle happens in the human body and soul. Fatigue sets in. Hunger grows. The soul, whether it admits it or not, yearns to breathe. And that's where God so often shows up—not in the thunder, but in the pause. The midday hour is more than just lunch—it's a divine checkpoint.

Jesus at the Well: A Midday Meeting That Changed a Life

There's a woman in John 4 whose entire life changed at 12 PM. We don't know her name, but we know her shame. We know her story because Jesus chose the middle of the day—the heat, the stillness, the quiet time when no one else would dare approach the well—to meet her.

"It was about the sixth hour." —John 4:6 (In Jewish timekeeping, the sixth hour is 12 noon)

The Samaritan woman came to draw water when the sun was at its harshest—likely to avoid the gossiping eyes and condemning whispers of the town's women. She was known, not for her piety, but for her broken past. Five husbands. Living with a sixth man who wasn't her husband. Rejected. Avoided. Alone.

But Jesus was waiting for her.

He sat at Jacob's well, wearied from His journey, but completely intentional in His purpose. He didn't go there for water. He went for her.

There, in the dry heat of midday, a thirsty soul met the Living Water.

What followed wasn't a sermon, but a conversation—a gentle unveiling of her story, her shame, and her potential. And in that exchange, she encountered the Messiah. A woman who came to draw water ended up dropping her jar and running into town with a message: *"Come, see a man who told me everything I ever did."* (John 4:29)

Midday became her moment of salvation, truth, and transformation.

The Sacred Pause: Reflection, Realignment, and Rest

It's easy to start the day well. Many rise early, pray, plan, and step into their responsibilities with purpose. But by noon, the day begins to unravel. The demands increase. The mind becomes crowded. Decisions weigh heavier. Emotions stir.

12 PM becomes a soul mirror.

- ✓ *How am I doing?*
- ✓ *Where have I drifted?*
- ✓ *Am I carrying more than I was meant to?*
- ✓ *Am I still walking with God—or just working for Him?*

This is where midday offers us a chance to reset.

In the Old Testament, David made it a point to pause three times a day to pray:

"Evening, and morning, and at noon I will pray, and cry aloud, and He shall hear my voice." —Psalm 55:17

He understood what many of us forget—noon is holy. It's not just a break from work. It's a moment to realign the soul, to let go of what's heavy, to re-center on what matters.

The very structure of the Hebrew day invited intentional pauses, not because God needed them, but because we do.

Midday Appointments: When God Interrupts Our Routine

Sometimes, God uses the 12 PM hour to do more than restore—He uses it to redirect.

In Acts 10, we find the apostle Peter on a rooftop around the sixth hour—again, 12 noon—waiting for lunch. But while his stomach hungered for food, God gave him a vision that would open the gospel to the Gentiles.

"Peter went up on the housetop to pray, about the sixth hour. Then he became very hungry and wanted to eat; but while they made ready, he fell into a trance…" —Acts 10:9–10

This wasn't coincidence. This was divine timing. Peter was in a place of prayer, rest, and stillness when God showed him the clean and the unclean animals, revealing the radical inclusivity of the gospel.

What if Peter had ignored that rooftop moment? What if he had rushed into a meeting or gotten lost in the busyness of the day? He might have missed one of the most significant turning points in church history.

Likewise, God often speaks in the margins—not just when we're praying, but when we're open. And 12 PM provides that sacred opening.

Real-Life Reflection: The Nurse in the Break Room

I remember speaking to a nurse named Maria who worked long, grueling shifts in a city hospital. She shared how her only consistent alone time was during her 30-minute lunch at noon. One day, emotionally drained and exhausted from tending to terminal patients, she went to the small break room and simply sat in silence.

She didn't plan to pray. She didn't even know what to say. But tears began to flow. And in that moment, she felt what she described as "a warm blanket of peace" wrap around her. She heard no voice. Saw no vision. But her soul exhaled. And that pause gave her strength to go back and serve with joy.

Since that day, she began calling 12 PM her "God moment." Every shift. Every day. No matter how small, she chose to meet Him in the middle—and He never failed to show up.

Why This Hour Still Matters

The 12 PM hour is not reserved for the super spiritual. It is God's invitation to everyone—no matter your profession or schedule—to stop and drink deeply from the well of grace.

It reminds us that God doesn't just move in cathedrals or early mornings. He's in the lunch breaks. The rooftop prayers. The ordinary hours made sacred by presence.

Jesus didn't meet the woman at the well at sunrise. He met her at **midday**, when the sun was merciless and she was emotionally empty. And that's often how He comes to us too—not when we feel spiritual, but when we feel dry, tired, or alone.

Closing Prayer: A Midday Meeting

Lord, here I am—in the middle of my day, in the middle of my thoughts, in the middle of my fatigue. Meet me at the well again. Remind me of who I am. Restore what the morning has drained. Realign me to Your pace and Your peace. Like the woman You met at noon, I open my heart for fresh water. Fill me again. Redirect me if I've drifted. And help me to see You even in the still moments. In Jesus' name, Amen.

Chapter 10:
3 PM – The Hour of Power

When Heaven Tore the Curtain

Time can be marked in seconds, minutes, and hours—but some hours shake eternity.

3 PM is one of them.

To the average person, 3 PM is simply a slump—the post-lunch haze, the edge of fatigue, the beginning of the late-day drag. But to those who understand the rhythm of God's timing, 3 PM is not a fading hour—it's a breakthrough hour.

- ✓ *It is the hour when the veil tore.*
- ✓ *It is the hour when the sky darkened.*
- ✓ *It is the hour when the earth trembled.*
- ✓ *It is the hour when Jesus cried out, "It is finished."*

The hour of **surrender**.

The hour of **salvation**.

The hour of **power.**

The Death of Jesus: The Hour That Changed the World

On a hill called Golgotha, nailed between two criminals, hung the innocent Lamb of God. From the sixth hour (12 PM) to the ninth hour (3 PM), the land was covered in darkness (Matthew 27:45). Not just cloud cover—but a divine eclipse of judgment, grief, and heaven's mourning.

And then, at exactly 3 PM, the silence broke:

"At about three in the afternoon Jesus cried out in a loud voice, 'Eli, Eli, lema sabachthani?' (which means 'My God, my God, why have You forsaken

Me?')"
—Matthew 27:46
And moments later, with a final breath, He declared:
"It is finished." —John 19:30
Not defeated. Not dismissed. Finished.
Sin paid for.
Shame removed.
The curtain between God and man forever torn.
"Then Jesus cried again with a loud voice and gave up His spirit. At that moment the curtain of the temple was torn in two, from top to bottom." —Matthew 27:50–51
That veil, which had separated man from the Holy of Holies for generations, didn't fall gently—it ripped. God Himself tore it from heaven downward, signifying that from that moment on, access to His presence was open.
And it happened at 3 PM—the ninth hour.

The Temple's Ninth-Hour Pattern
This hour wasn't randomly chosen. According to Jewish tradition, 3 PM (the ninth hour) was the time of the evening sacrifice and prayer in the temple. It was a sacred, ordained moment, where incense was offered, prayers were lifted, and the people sought the mercy of God.
"Now Peter and John went up together to the temple at the hour of prayer, the ninth hour." —Acts 3:1
It was during this sacred hour that they encountered a lame man at the temple gate—and God's power moved.
Peter, filled with the Spirit, declared:
"Silver and gold I do not have, but what I do have I give you. In the name of Jesus Christ of Nazareth, rise up and walk." —Acts 3:6

A man who had never walked leapt up with strength. Why? Because the ninth hour is not just the hour of prayer—it is the hour of power. Miracles. Movement. Mercy. These weren't limited to temple rituals. They had now become available to all who believed in the risen Christ.

3 PM Today: Still an Hour of Miracles, Salvation, and Healing

The power of 3 PM wasn't confined to the cross or the temple. It is still available today—for those who pause, who lean in, who pray not from routine, but from expectancy.

There's something sacred that happens when we pray at 3 PM—not because the hour itself is magical, but because we're aligning ourselves with a moment where heaven has historically moved.

Throughout history, revivals and spiritual awakenings have been sparked by people who learned to pray with the rhythms of God.

I once met a woman whose son had been estranged for years—lost in addiction, bitterness, and rebellion. She told me, *"Every day at 3 PM, I would stop whatever I was doing and whisper his name to Jesus."*

Years went by. Nothing changed. But she never missed the hour. She said, "If Jesus gave everything at that hour, then I will give Him this small offering of faith each day."

One day, her son walked through the front door—sober, broken, and asking to be prayed for.

God heard.

God moved.

Because 3 PM is not too late in the day—it's often right on time for a miracle.

Surrendered Power: The Paradox of the Cross

There's a divine paradox at the heart of 3 PM. The hour when Jesus looked His weakest was, in reality, His greatest moment of power.

He was mocked. Bleeding. Abandoned.

But that cry—*"It is finished"*—was not a whisper of defeat. It was a roar of authority.

Hell was shaken.

Sin was shattered.

Death was dethroned.

This reminds us that the greatest power often comes not in moments of triumph, but in moments of surrender.

The 3 PM hour invites us into that same paradox. It's not a time to grasp for control—but to release it. To surrender the weight of our day, our failures, our longings—to the One who already finished the work.

When we surrender at 3 PM, we don't weaken. We step into resurrection power.

A Call to Remember, Realign, and Release

Imagine what could happen if people across the world paused at 3 PM each day—not for tradition, but for transformation.

What if every hospital room, classroom, office, and home became a sacred space at that hour?

What if our phones reminded us to stop—not to scroll, but to speak to the Father?

What if we chose to kneel, even if just in our hearts, to honor the hour that split history in two?

You don't need a liturgy. Just a willing heart.

At 3 PM, the heavens are already open. You're not earning access—you're stepping into it.

Closing Prayer: The Veil Is Torn

Jesus, at 3 PM You gave it all. You held nothing back. You surrendered so I could be set free. Now I come to You—midday burdens in hand, wounds exposed, questions still raw. I remember what You did. I receive what You offer. And I rest in the finished work of the cross. Tear through anything in me that still hides behind a veil. Let this hour be holy again. Let miracles flow, healing come, and salvation spring forth. Because of You, I can come boldly. And I do—right now. In Your powerful name, Amen.

Appendices

Appendix A: Daily Prayer Guide (By Hour)

Simple Devotionals & Decrees for Sacred Alignment
Time is holy when it is surrendered to God. While our clocks may tick on with mechanical precision, the spirit responds to the rhythm of heaven. Below is a practical guide that aligns your heart with the Father at the sacred corner hours: 6 PM, 9 PM, 12 AM, 3 AM, 6 AM, 9 AM, 12 PM, and 3 PM—moments marked by divine encounter throughout Scripture. You can use this guide daily as a brief devotional prayer, decree, or reflection to honor these sacred moments.

---

6 PM – The Divine Reset
"And there was evening and there was morning—the first day." (Genesis 1:5)
Reflection:
As the biblical day begins at sundown, 6 PM is the divine threshold—a sacred invitation to lay down the burdens of the past and enter God's rhythm of rest and trust.
Prayer/Decree:
"Lord, as this biblical day begins, I choose to enter Your rest. I let go of every burden, failure, and fear. Reset my soul. I declare that this evening ushers in renewal, clarity, and peace. In Jesus' name."

---

9 PM – The Night Watch
"But at midnight Paul and Silas were praying and singing hymns…" (Acts 16:25)
Reflection:
The first watch of the night calls us to vigilance,

meditation, and prayerful surrender. This is the hour when heaven listens as saints lay down their hearts in trust.

Prayer/Decree:

"Father, as the world quiets, I tune my heart to Your whisper. Guard my dreams and my rest. I cover my household under the blood of Jesus. I decree that angels encamp around me tonight."

---

12 AM – The Midnight Cry

"At midnight a cry rang out: 'Here is the bridegroom!'" (Matthew 25:6)

Reflection:

The midnight hour is both mysterious and mighty. It is the hour of visitation, breakthrough, and intercession. A time when the veil thins and heaven moves powerfully.

Prayer/Decree:

"Lord, I lift up my cry at midnight. I intercede for my family, my city, and my calling. May deliverance arise. Let every chain break. I decree victory and supernatural intervention in the mighty name of Jesus."

---

3 AM – The Fourth Watch

"About the fourth watch of the night He came to them, walking on the sea." (Mark 6:48)

Reflection:

The fourth watch is the most spiritually sensitive hour. Many awaken at this time with dreams or burdens. It is when Jesus walked on water, bringing peace to the storm.

Prayer/Decree:

"Holy Spirit, I invite You to speak in the silence. I yield my heart to Your leading. Let every storm

around me be calmed. I declare prophetic clarity, peace, and supernatural direction."

---

6 AM – Morning with the Master
"Very early in the morning… Jesus went off to pray." (Mark 1:35)
Reflection:
Morning holds promise. With the sunrise comes new mercy, fresh strength, and clarity. It's the hour Jesus met with the Father to align His mission for the day.
Prayer/Decree:
"Father, I offer this day to You. Thank You for Your new mercies. I commit every task, every decision, every word to You. Order my steps. I decree divine alignment today."

---

9 AM – The Spirit Hour
"These are not drunk as you suppose, since it is only the third hour." (Acts 2:15)
Reflection:
This was the hour of Pentecost—when the Spirit descended and birthed the Church. 9 AM is a time of empowerment and spiritual boldness.
Prayer/Decree:
"Holy Spirit, fill me afresh. Let Your power rest upon me. Use me today as Your vessel. I decree wisdom, discernment, and boldness in all I do."

---

12 PM – The Hour of Encounter
"It was about noon, and Jesus, tired as He was, sat down by the well." (John 4:6)
Reflection:
Midday is the hour of personal encounters. A time to pause, reflect, and reset. The Samaritan woman met Christ at this hour, and her life was never the same.

Prayer/Decree:

"Jesus, I pause to meet You again. Realign my heart, remove distractions, and refill my spirit. I decree divine appointments and personal revival."

---

3 PM – The Hour of Power

"At three in the afternoon, Jesus cried out… and gave up His spirit." (Matthew 27:46, 50)

Reflection:

This is the hour the veil tore. A time of divine exchange. When surrender unlocked supernatural access.

Prayer/Decree:

"Lord, I remember Your finished work. I surrender again. Let healing flow, let salvation visit every soul I'm praying for. I decree open heavens and miracle encounters now."

Appendix B:
Biblical Timeline Table of Events by Hour

A Chronological Look at Sacred Timings in Scripture
Time in the Bible is not random. Throughout both Old and New Testaments, God moved powerfully at set hours, many of which correspond with the four corner hours we've explored—6, 9, 12, 3—whether morning or night. This timeline reveals how heaven consistently met earth at these hours, providing a prophetic pattern for us to follow today.

Biblical Events by Hour

Hour	Event	Scripture Reference	Spiritual Significance
6 PM (Evening)	God begins each day at evening	Genesis 1:5	Start your day with rest and trust
9 PM	Daniel prayed during evening sacrifice	Daniel 9:21	Night watch intercession and angelic visitation
12 AM	Paul and Silas worshipped in prison	Acts 16:25	Worship in warfare brings breakthrough
3 AM	Jesus walks on water (4th watch)	Mark 6:48	Peace in the storm; divine presence
6 AM	Jesus rises	Mark 1:35	New mercies,

Hour	Event	Scripture Reference	Spiritual Significance
	early to pray		daily surrender
9 AM	Holy Spirit descends at Pentecost	Acts 2:15	Power to live and witness
12 PM	Jesus meets Samaritan woman	John 4:6	Personal revival and life change
3 PM	Jesus dies; veil torn	Matthew 27:46–51	Finished work, access to the Father

Conclusion

We began this journey with a clock and a question. Why do so many clocks mark only four numbers—12, 3, 6, and 9? Why do these hours keep appearing in Scripture? And what would it mean to live in step with heaven's time?

As we've discovered through the pages of this book, these corner hours are not empty points on a dial—they are divine appointments. Sacred markers. Holy ground disguised as ordinary time.

From 6 PM's divine reset, to 3 AM's spiritual clarity, to 3 PM's hour of mercy and power, we find that God has been present in time all along—waiting for us not just to pray occasionally, but to walk daily in rhythm with Him.

This is more than a spiritual routine. It's a realignment of our lives with the ways of God. It's about surrendering the clock, not to chaos, but to Christ. It's about recovering the lost art of watchfulness, and remembering that the veil was torn at an appointed hour—so we could boldly step in, any time, with confidence and intimacy.

This sacred pattern—prayer, presence, power, and peace—can transform families, cities, even nations. And it starts with just one person choosing to honor God in time.

So as you close this book, let me encourage you:
Don't just return to your schedule.
Return to the sacred.
Let the hour lead you to prayer.
Let the rhythm remind you to rest.
Let the interruptions become invitations.

Let the day begin at evening, in trust, and end at morning, in praise.
Because from evening to morning, He is God.
And from this hour forward, so may He be your Lord of time.
Amen.

About the Author 'GERARD ASSEY'

Gerard Assey is a Graduate in Economics, a PGD in Management (HRD) and holds a Doctorate in Leadership. Gerard holds several International Qualifications in Sales, Debt Collection, Training & Teaching, and is a 'Fellow' of the prestigious 'Institute of Sales & Marketing Management'-UK, a Certified NLP Practitioner, a 'Certified Trainer', an 'Accredited Management Teacher-Behavioral Sciences', a 'Certified Competency Facilitator', a 'Certified Management Consultant'- (the International credentials of a professional management consultant, awarded in accordance with global standards of the ICMCI); and a Certification from the University of Michigan in 'Successful Negotiation: Essential Strategies and Skills'

He is also a Member of the 'National Association of Sales Professionals' backed with several years experience in varied industries, both in India and Overseas. He also holds an 'Etiquette Consultant' Certification from the USA (by Sue Fox, Author of Best Seller: 'Business Etiquette for Dummies'. She has trained some of the top celebrities' world over). He was also a recipient of a scholarship for extensive training in Japan on 'Corporate Management for India'.

Gerard Assey is 'Founder & Chief Corporate Trainer' of the Group: '**Citius, Altius, Fortius Unlimited'**- an organization that **celebrated 20 years of Glorious Service** in 2021, focusing on 3 Core Competencies:

People. Performance. Profit; in functional areas of Sales & Marketing, HR & Organizational Development, covering Recruitment, Training & Consultancy!

Having managed organizations with large Sales Forces in India & Overseas, his specialization cover extensive areas of Sales Training (All levels - Presentation, Negotiation, Key/ Strategic Accounts Management & Managerial Skills for all sectors), Bid Proposal/ Capture Planning/ Management Trainings, Retail Sales, Customer Service & Customer Retention Programs, Training for Prevention & Collection of Debt, Self & Personal Development Programs (Time Management, Teamwork & Team Building, Business Etiquette & Personal Grooming, Leadership & Managerial Skills, People Management Skills, Train-the-Trainer etc), including preparation of Custom-designed Business Manuals for Internal (HR, Induction, and Sales etc) & External use (Instruction, User Manuals).

Gerard has successfully conducted over 6460 Trainings & Workshops (as of June '25) all across India, Middle East, Africa, Europe & S.E. Asia. Besides public programs conducted regularly, both in India & Overseas, he has some of the top names as clients whom he services from Single Owners to large Public & Government undertakings, covering all sectors, for their in-house needs.

His website: www.CollectionSkills.com is the only one in this part of the world to be featured in the 'Collections & Credit Risk Magazine-USA' under 'Who's Who in Training' and ranks TOP, along with other websites listed below on most search engines.

Gerard is author of 197 books already (July 2025), all the books being available on all online platforms and outlets as E-books and Paperbacks

A few of our business related books:

1. Bite-sized Bits on Commonsense Management
2. Heart to Heart on Life's Principles'
3. How to become a Successful Manager
4. The Sales Professionals' Master Workbook of S.Y.S.T.E.M.S
5. The Professional Business Email Etiquette Handbook & Guide
6. The Professional Business Video-Conferencing Etiquette Handbook & Guide
7. Professional Presentation Skills
8. Exceptional Customer Service
9. Professional Tele-Marketing Skills
10. Professional Debt Collection Skills
11. The G.R.E.A.T. Sales & Service Workbook
12. Sales Training Advantage for Results (*The Ultimate Sales Training Manual to enable you stand out as a S.T.A.R.*)
13. CEO Daily Planner & Organizer
14. The Sales Professionals' Master Daily Planner
15. The Professional Debt Collector's Master Daily Planner
16. My Daily Planner & Organizer
17. MY EMERGENCY INFORMATION RECORD (Family Emergency & Peace of Mind Planner)
18. The Ultimate Therapist & Counselors Planner and Organizer
19. Building an Ethical Workplace
20. Managing Relationships at Work
21. Managing Business Meetings Effectively
22. Effective Delegation Skills
23. Goal Setting for Success
24. B2B Selling by Email
25. Professional Business Etiquette & Grooming
26. Dining Etiquette & Table Manners
27. Effective Networking Skills
28. Grooming, Etiquette & Manners for Teens, Young Adults & Future Leaders
29. Inter-Personal Skills
30. Get Ready, Get Hired!
31. Selling in a Recession
32. Effective Receivables Management in an Economic Downturn!
33. Real Estate & Property Sales Training
34. Credit Sales & Accounts Receivable Management

35. Selling Skills for Real Estate & Property Advisors
36. Take G.R.E.A.T. C.A.R.E!
37. Spa, Salon & Health Club Selling Skills
38. Selling Travel, Holiday & MICE Services
39. Selling Skills for Spa's, Salons & Health Clubs
40. Retailing in Salons & Spas
41. Selling Holiday, Vacation, Tours & Packages
42. The Power of Sales Referrals
43. Selling Luxury
44. Technical Selling Skills
45. Financial Advisors Sales Training
46. Dealing with Burnout at Work Monopolize Your Markets
47. Selling to Affluent Customers
48. Growing up with Grace
49. Financial Selling Skills
50. *The Effective Manager's Guide: Key Skills to Thrive*
51. From Aspiring to Inspiring: A Guide for New Managers on the Rise
52. The Power of Focus
53. Selling with Integrity: Sell Like Jesus The Perfect Role Model!
54. 31 Habits of Champions: Your 31-Day Journey to Greatness
55. Rejecting Grasshopper Talk: From Grasshopper to Giant-Killer-*Defeating Giants Daily!*
56. Navigate the AI-Powered Future of Bid & Proposals: Up-Skill to Stay Relevant with Alternative Career Paths & Opportunities
57. Hiring Sales Winners
58. Present with Impact
59. Success Unlocked: *Breaking Free from Habits that Hold You Back*
60. Complaints to Cheers, Feedback to Gold: Mastering Complaints Management
61. Thriving Together: *Cultivating Diversity, Equity, and Inclusion*
62. Coaching Skills for Sales Managers
63. Soaring to Success in Business & Leadership: Swifter, Higher, Stronger!
64. From Classroom to Podium: A Student's Guide to Powerful Public Speaking & Presentation Skills
65. Developing Self-Discipline
66. The CEO's 31-Day Power Plan: Unlocking Success through Essential Traits

67. Credibility Matters
68. A Winning Attitude
69. Bid & Proposal Management Using AI
70. Sales Forecasting: A Practical & Proven Guide to Strategic Sales Forecasting
71. Elevate & Energize: *50 Dynamic & Fun Activities for Peak Workplace Morale*
72. 'Sales SOS! Sales on Fire! *30 Days to Conquer Chaos & the Nightmares of Success!'*
73. Mastering Sales Managerial Skills: *Building High-Performing Teams & Driving Exceptional Results*
74. Eagle-Eyed Leadership: Unleashing the Power of 31 Lessons from Eagles
75. The Ultimate Employee Training Guide: *Training Today, Leading Tomorrow*
76. Being More Accountable at Work
77. Creating a Culture of Continuous Improvement
78. Effective Questioning & Listening Skills
79. The Power of Value Selling
80. The Growth Mindset
81. Mastering Professional Help Desk Skills
82. The Power to Lead with Empathy
83. Being Prepared: The Key to Unlocking Success
84. Youthful Spark-Youth Energizers, Activities and Games-Igniting the Fun in Youth
85. Ignite your Motivation for Success
86. Elevate Your Executive Presence: *Your Roadmap to Executive Excellence*
87. Smart Decisions: *Mastering Problem Solving with Strategic Solutions for Business Success*
88. Strategic Planning: *Developing and Implementing Strategic Plans to Achieve Long-Term Business Goals*
89. The Power of Stay Interviews
90. Developing G.R.I.T.
91. Adaptability
92. Diagnosis- *A Key Skill for Leadership*
93. The Burnout-Proof Salesperson: *The Master Guide to Preventing Stress & Burnout-* Strategies for Thriving in Sales
94. Learning from Failure: *Keys to Success*
95. Customer Success Management
96. Overcoming the Killers of Motivation
97. The C-Suite Code: *Mastering Skills for Executive Excellence'*

98. Dealing with Difficult Customers
99. Unlocking Your Potential: Mastering the Top 20 Life Skills for a Brighter Future
100. Nurturing Tomorrow's Leaders: *Essential Soft Skills Every Child Must Learn*
101. Lively & Fun Party Games for Seniors & Elders
102. Role Playing for Sales Champions: From Practice to Performance
103. Fun and Exciting Party Games for Kids
104. Case Studies for Sales
105. Role-Playing for Unbeatable Customer Service
106. Case Studies in Customer Service
107. Case Studies in Winning Negotiations
108. Case Studies in Management & Leadership
109. Case Studies in Human Resources & Talent Management
110. CEO Success Blueprint: The Essential Toolkit for CEOs and C-Level Executives
111. The Salesperson's Self-Coaching Guide: *Master Your Own Self-Coaching Plan for Success*
112. Overcoming Procrastination: *Your Ultimate Guide to Stop Delaying and Start Living Your Best Life*
113. When True Colors Are Exposed: *The Journey to Unmasking Humanity*
114. Life-Changing Habits for Teens: Teen Success Blueprint for a Bright Future
115. Workplace Stress-Free: *Proven Strategies to Thrive at Work and Beyond*
116. Objection Overruled: *The Ultimate Guide to Turning 'No' into 'Yes'"*
117. Building Strong Teams: *A Comprehensive Guide to Team Building*
118. Ethical & Moral Leadership in Business: *Eliminating Unethical Practices & Building a Culture of Trust & Integrity*
119. Rising Strong: Building Positive: High Self-Esteem for a Fulfilling Life-*A Practical Guide for Students, Employees, Leaders & Entrepreneurs*

From the Ministry side, Gerard graduated in the very first batch of Charis Bible College-India & had for over 9 years served as a Part-time Faculty at Charis Bible College-Chennai (Andrew Wommack Ministries-Colorado, USA). He also holds a Diploma in Worship (a subject closest to his heart) from the JSOW and is also a graduate of the Advanced Mentorship Program (AMP) and the Circle Of Ministerial Engagement (C.O.M.E.) of Prophet Jerome Fernando and a Spiritual Son of the Esteemed Prophet. An accomplished author of several Secular & Christian Books, Gerard has been on the board of a few international organizations and boasts of being the SON of the MOST HIGH GOD: An ordinary guy following an extraordinary GOD!

...And some of his most recent Christian Books being:

1. A Bouquet of Praises for My KING
2. Christian Jokes for the Serious Religious' Folks!
3. Jesus Healed You!
4. Praise24Ever! (also in Tamil version)
5. The 5G Network of GOD
6. Building Faith over F.E.A.R- FACE EVERYTHING AND RISE with JESUS
7. Hebrew and Greek Praise and Worship Words
8. Godly Mothers' and Grandmothers' Bible Story time for Kids!
9. Miracles of Jesus in Pictures
10. Raise your Praise all 365 Days
11. Thanking GOD with an Attitude of Gratitude
12. Meditating on the Attributes of GOD
13. Puppet Scripts
14. Alcohol Ruins, JESUS Reforms, Renews & Restores!
15. Habakkuk 2:2 Christian Daily Journal, Planner & Organizer
16. ABC of GOD's Word for Handwriting Practice
17. Daily Bible Verse Handwriting Practice (Building Godly Character & Faith through Cursive Handwriting Practice!)
18. Guiding Light: Fun & Faith-Building Bible Activities for Children
19. Rejecting Grasshopper Talk: From Grasshopper to Giant-Killer-*Defeating Giants Daily!*
20. Teen Titans of Faith: *Building Courage, Determination & Christ-like-Esteem*
21. I AM Empowered: *Unleashing Divine Power with Positive Declarations*
22. Be A Solution Provider-*From Passion to Purpose*: *A Biblical Guide to Being the Answer to the World!*
23. Miracles of JESUS
24. Parables of Jesus for a Meaningful Life!

25. A Grateful Heart: Importance of Sharing Testimonies of GOD's Grace
26. Melodies of Worship to JESUS: 31 Songs of Praise & Worship From My Heart to HIS!
27. I AM SO BLESSED!
28. My Daily Cup of Energizer
29. 31 Leadership Lessons *from* Jesus- *The Supreme Leader*
30. Peace Amidst Storms: A Biblical Guide to Conquering S.T.R.E.S.S.
31. Rise Above: 20 Biblical Eagle Lessons for Life's Triumphs
32. Godly Goal Setting: *The FAITHFUL Blueprint for a Purpose-Driven Life*
33. The Profound Attributes of our Mighty GOD: Understanding the 10S's of the Almighty
34. Worship Now, Worship Forever: *A Journey from Earthly Praise to Eternal Glory*
35. Unceasing Praise & Worship: *365 Days to Worship the King*
36. The ROAR Within: *Living with Purpose and Authority through the Power of the Holy Spirit*
37. From Potential to Purpose: Unlocking and Multiplying Your Talents & Gifts for Kingdom Impact
38. Songs from the Heart: *Worshipping GOD in Your Own Tune & Melody*
39. Awakening Praise & Worship: Hebrew & Greek Words to Raise Your Praise
40. Sing a NEW Song to the LORD Everyday: *Daily Devotions of Praise & Worship to Lift Your Heart & Glorify HIS Name*
41. *The* A.R.O.M.A. of True Worship: *Creating Worship That Delights God*
42. Becoming A Kingdom Champion: *Embracing God's Call for a Life of Purpose & Victory*
43. The Busy Businessman's Daily Devotional: 366 Crisp Truths to Start Your Day Strong
44. The Teacher's Heart: *Daily Devotions for Educators*
45. Anchored! *A 31-Day Devotional for Students Facing Life's Challenges*
46. Suddenly! Unlocking Unorthodox Breakthroughs through Unusual Worship
47. Overcoming Adversity: *Lessons from the Bible for Modern Challenges*
48. LORD, Don't do it without me
49. Kingdom Leadership: *Biblical Principles for Modern Leaders*
50. Heartprints of God- *Growing God's Way:* Daily Devotions for Kids to Shine Bright

51. Send Judah First: Let your Praises Go up First to See the Mighty Move of GOD
52. DIVINE MOMENTS: *Recognizing, Embracing, Preparing, and Walking into Life-Changing Encounters with God*
53. Be a Builder in the Kingdom: *The C.E.M.E.N.T. Guide to Creating a Lasting Legacy*
54. Unshakable: *Pillars of Godly Womanhood*
    (Pillars of Faith That Changed History)
55. Lead Like a Shepherd: *14 Essential Traits for Pastoral Excellence*
56. The Worship Leader's Arsenal: *Powerful Exhortations to Ignite Thanksgiving, Praise & Worship*
57. Women of UnShakable Faith: *31-Day Devotional for Strength, Purpose & Influence*
58. Called to Teach: *A Complete 10-Week Training Guide for Impactful VBS Teachers*
59. Strumming for the KING: Cowboy Songs of Faith & Fire
60. The Ultimate Youth Camp Playbook: *50 Bible-Centered Indoor Games to Engage, Equip, and Empower Teens*
61. Glad in HIS Presence: *David's Revelation of GOD's Love & Mercy*
62. The Spirit Behind the Sound: *52 Devotionals for Worship Teams*
63. THE COWBOY'S COMPASS: *Riding the Trail of Faith with Grit & Grace*
64. Worship as My Weapon: *Living Victoriously through the Power of Praise*
65. A Worshipper Always Wins: *Living a Life of Victorious Worship*
66. Worship That Leads to the Throne: *Practical Strategies for Worship Leaders to Inspire Their Team & Usher People into God's Presence*
67. Worship as Warfare: *Conquering through the Sound of Surrender*
68. Watchmen on the Walls: *A 31-Day Devotional for Worship Teams*
69. KINGDOM BUSINESS: *52 Biblical Principles for GODLY Leadership & Wise Decisions*
70. From Evening to Morning: *Rediscovering GOD's Sacred Hours*

Besides regularly contributing to business & trade journals, including international ones such as the 'Creative Training Techniques' and the 'Sales News' of the U.S.A, He is also a member of several prestigious bodies & trade associations, having participated in many Conferences & Workshops in India & Overseas.

Prior to his last assignment of leading & managing a large MNC as head, Gerard had a 3-year stint in the Middle East as a Consultant with a leading British Consultancy Firm.

As the past 'Official Country Representative' for the International Business Award- 'THE STEVIES'-(the business world's own Oscar) for about 4 years- he ensured a few Indian companies that qualify for the same every year!

Gerard can be contacted at:
Email: training@Sales-Training.in,training@CollectionSkills.com
Websites:

www.Sales-Training.in
www.EtiquetteWorks.in
www.CollectionSkills.com
www.RetailSalesTraining.in
www.SalesTrainingIndia.com
www.ManualPreparation.com
www.TrainingWithPuppets.com
www.FirstContactAcademy.com
www.SalesAndMarketingRecruiter.com

www.ingramcontent.com/pod-product-compliance
Ingram Content Group UK Ltd.
Pitfield, Milton Keynes, MK11 3LW, UK
UKHW021341190726
13845UKWH00027B/664

9 788198 697431